Short Stack Editions | Volume 15

Summer Squash

by Sarah Baird

Short Stack Editions

Publisher: Nick Fauchald
Creative Director: Rotem Raffe
Editor: Kaitlyn Goalen
Copy Editor: Abby Tannenbaum
Director of Development: Mackenzie Smith

Published in the United States by All Day Press (AllDayPress.com).

ISBN 978-0-9907853-4-7

Printed in New York City
May 2015

Table of Contents

Raw

Baked

Fried

Stovetop

When we created Short Stack Editions,

we wanted to feature all kinds of ingredients: fresh produce, pantry staples, meat and more. But the model for Short Stacks really shines with an ingredient like summer squash.

This poetic fruit (yes, it's actually a fruit!) is a tidal wave. For just a few months of the year, summer squash is everywhere, rampantly and widely available. Such a bumper crop requires creative reinforcements in the kitchen and, each summer, after exhausting our standby squash recipes in just a few weeks, we're desperate for new and exciting ways to put it to use.

This very kind of urgent need, sparked from our intense love for an ingredient, grew into the idea for this series.

And this edition, expertly written and developed by Sarah Baird, has lived up to every hope we had when we set out to make these books. Her recipes jump the tracks of genre, exposing squash's unending versatility. But Sarah also pays careful homage to specific varietals within the squash family, honing in on the nuances that make us more intuitive as cooks.

Armed with Sarah's witty prose and inventive, delicious recipes, we're entering squash season with newfound excitement. We hope that this collection has the same effect in your kitchen.

—*The Editors*

2

Introduction

I used summer squash long before I understood how to cook with it. Every summer as a child, I spent hours in my grandfather's garden figuring out just how many imaginative functions the overflow of summer squash could perform. In the mind of an eight-year-old, squash blossoms were tiny houses for june bugs, while zucchini were plump wands with which to conduct my invisible garden orchestra. When I dressed up for a tea party, squash vines and tendrils became my jewelry: winding, curlicue bracelets and necklaces gifted from the earth.

Above all else, I learned to respect summer squash as the kind of plant that's both malleable and generous, giving of itself in a way that's infinitely adaptable and exceedingly openhanded. It was extra special, then, when I discovered that summer squash was also delicious, bringing the same canvas for innovation and imagination to the kitchen that it did in the wild.

Each year, so many of my farmers' market-frequenting friends heave and set, groaning over the glut of summer squash taking up space in lieu of more exotic produce selections. Me? I relish it. Although the majority of summer squash consumed in the United States is actually indigenous, squash remains one of the few ingredients that's truly cross-cultural and a touchstone for exploring new flavors, textures and cuisines.

But much like a British period-drama character prone to fainting spells, squash is the kind of ingredient that can easily be overwhelmed. I was determined to not let that happen with any of the recipes in this book. The result? All the recipes—except lamb-stuffed pattypan—are vegetarian, and a number are either vegan or raw. This was quite a happy accident (my freezer, chock full of elk, wild boar and deer meat, proves that I am assuredly a meat eater). There's never a spot in the book where squash isn't given its moment in the sun, collaborating only with ingredients that allow it to glow with greater intensity instead of attempting to hide its light. (This is also probably good relationship advice.)

Due to their meat-free status, many of the recipes here can satisfy almost anyone (including skeptical omnivores) and will help your next food-driven soiree go off without a hitch. There's the zucchini not-so-Bloody Mary for your pal who arrives at brunch fresh from Pilates seeking a vegan, green (but still boozy) drink. The rib-sticking Hungarian squash casserole and biscuit-topped squash cobbler will woo guests who seek comfort food. Squash blossom soup that will refresh you on a melting July day: Check. A downright regal raw squash and carrot "ceviche" that makes a stunning centerpiece? You're covered.

Whether it's conjuring up the garden patch playfulness of neighborhood children or anchoring your dinner table, summer squash is a faithful friend that will continue to both hearten and challenge our palates with unmatched freshness.

—Sarah Baird

Recipes

Types of Summer Squash

The squash varieties used in this book's recipes are largely interchangeable, except when form and function—like stuffing a pattypan—deem one more practical than another. However, the world of summer squash (something we all probably feel we know by heart) is far more complex and intricate than it appears at first blush. Here's a quick primer on our garden bounty heroes.

Yellow Summer Squash

Aliases: Crookneck squash, straightneck squash

Shape: The classic oblong squash of our childhoods, yellow summer squash possesses a plump body and either a slightly hooked or straight neck.

Color: Light to sunshine-y yellow

Siblings: The Zephyr squash, which has been bred to be two-tone green and yellow

Spirit Animal: Golden retriever

Zucchini

Alias: Courgette

Shape: Oblong and cylindrical, the zucchini can be slightly curved, lumpy or stick straight.

Color: Emerald green, forest green, green striped

Siblings: Golden zucchini, a hybrid creation that's yellow or burnt orange in color

Spirit Animal: Gecko

Gem Squash

Alias: Rondini

Shape: Spherical and solid, the gem squash grows to the size of a softball.

Color: Hunter green

Spirit Animal: Armadillo

Pattypan Squash

Aliases: Scallop squash, granny squash, custard squash

Shape: Petite (2 to 3 inches) and flying-saucer-shaped, the pattypan's most endearing trait is its delicate scalloped edges.

Color: A full spectrum of green, white, yellow and cream hues

Spirit Animal: Box turtle

Eight-Ball Squash

Aliases: Round zucchini, roly-poly

Shape: Round, like a plump ball

Color: Deep, rich emerald green

Siblings: One-ball squash, which is yellow and often slightly smaller

Spirit Animal: Hedgehog

Squash Blossoms

Aliases: Zucchini flowers, squash flowers

Shape: Five-point, single-bud blooms

Color: Sunburst yellow, golden

Spirit Insect: Common birdwing butterfly

Chow Chow

A stalwart Appalachian condiment, chow chow is a finely minced pickled-vegetable relish that walks the line between tangy and sweet in each zippy bite. For gardeners faced with the daunting task of tackling a late-summer squash surplus, chow chow can quickly become a lifesaver. The dish allows an abundance of vegetable riches to achieve longevity as a concoction to savor year-round with pork chops, cornbread or slathered on a hot dog.

- ⅔ pound tomatillos, minced (about 2 cups)
- 1⅓ pounds summer squash, minced (about 4 cups)
- 1 pound red onions, minced (about 3 cups)
- ½ a head cauliflower, minced (about 1 cup)
- 1 jalapeño, seeded and minced
- ¼ cup kosher salt
- ¼ cup spice blend (recipe follows)
- 1½ cups apple cider vinegar
- 1½ cups raw sugar

Place the minced vegetables in a colander over a sink or large bowl and toss with the salt, mixing until well combined. Let the vegetables rest overnight, allowing excess water to drain off. Rinse the vegetables thoroughly and gently, removing any excess salt. Pat dry.

Place the spice blend in a square of cheesecloth and secure with a piece of string to make a small pouch. In a large heavy-bottomed pot, combine the vinegar and sugar and bring to a boil. Add the vegetables and spice bag.

Reduce the heat to medium and cook until the vegetables become tender and start to form a slurry, about 40 minutes.

Remove the spice bag and ladle the chow chow into airtight glass jars (such as Mason jars), filling each jar about three-quarters full. Chow chow will keep, refrigerated, for up to a week. Alternatively, seal the jars using the boiling water method, which will allow the chow chow to keep for up to 18 months (or indefinitely) if stored in a cool, dry place.

Spice Blend

- 1 cinnamon stick, halved
- 3 bay leaves, torn
- 2 teaspoons ground turmeric
- 2 teaspoons yellow mustard seeds
- 1 teaspoon whole juniper berries
- 2 teaspoons coriander seeds
- 2 teaspoons celery seeds
- 1 teaspoon black peppercorns
- 1 teaspoon dill seeds

Place all the ingredients in a lidded jar and shake to combine.

Zucchini Kimchi

Kimchi has always seemed magical to me. The spicy Korean dish stole my heart with my very first bite and led me skipping gleefully down a rabbit hole full of even more robust dishes. Squash is the perfect conduit for kimchi's tongue-singeing flavors, and anchovy paste adds a touch of brininess to the umami one-two punch. If you want to mix it up, try replacing the anchovy paste with shrimp paste or adding ½ cup of sliced scallions.

1 pound zucchini, sliced into ½-inch-thick rounds (about 3 cups)

½ pound radishes, sliced into matchsticks (about ½ cup)

2 tablespoons salt

2 teaspoons minced garlic

1 teaspoon minced ginger

1 teaspoon anchovy paste

3 teaspoons Sambal Oelek chili paste

½ teaspoon Gochujang flakes (or red pepper flakes)

½ teaspoon brown sugar

½ cup rice wine vinegar

Place the zucchini and radish in a colander over a sink or large bowl and toss with the salt, mixing until well combined. Let the vegetables rest for 3 to 4 hours, allowing excess water to drain off. Rinse the vegetables thoroughly and gently, removing any excess salt. Pat dry.

While the zucchini and radishes are draining, combine the garlic, ginger, anchovy paste, chili paste, chile flakes and sugar in a medium bowl. Add the vinegar and mix until completely incorporated.

Wring out any excess water from the vegetables by placing them in a clean kitchen towel and folding it into a roll. Hold on to both ends of the towel and twist to squeeze out the excess water. Add the vegetables to the marinade.

Store in an airtight glass jar (such as a Mason jar) and let stand at room temperature for 3 days. Shake the jar daily to make sure the zucchini slices are completely submerged. After 3 days, taste to ensure that the kimchi is spicy enough for you. If not, let the jar sit at room temperature for another 24 hours. Refrigerate for at least 1 day before serving. Although diehards say that technically kimchi can keep forever, it's safest to make another batch after 2 weeks.

Zucchini Benedictine Spread

Horses to the gate! The savory treat of choice for the Kentucky Derby is the Benedictine sandwich, or two pieces of white bread filled with a spread that is traditionally comprised of cucumber and cream cheese. At first blush, this dish may appear underwhelming, but with the right secret ingredients (hint: Worcestershire, hot sauce), this Bluegrass State classic is a come-from-behind winner.

The following is a more modern take on the traditional Benedictine recipe, replacing cucumber with zucchini and keeping the textural elements of the vegetables intact while adding in two kicks of hot sauce.

makes 2 cups

½ medium Vidalia onion, roughly chopped

2 medium zucchini (about ⅔ pound)—peeled, halved and seeded

8 ounces cream cheese, softened

¼ cup sour cream

1 tablespoon mayonnaise

1 tablespoon Worcestershire sauce

½ teaspoon salt

1 teaspoon hot sauce

1 teaspoon adobo sauce (from a can of chipotles in adobo)

Combine the onion and zucchini in a food processor and pulse until finely chopped.

Transfer the vegetable mixture to a fine-mesh strainer lined with cheesecloth. Using a spatula (or your hands), press down on the solids until the remaining water drains from the vegetables.

In large mixing bowl, combine the drained vegetables with the remaining ingredients. Whisk until completely combined. Cover and refrigerate for 2 hours to set. Serve the mixture with crackers or crudité, or layer between slices of white bread, tea-sandwich style. The spread can be refrigerated for up to 3 days.

Selecting Summer Squash

It can be tempting to reach for the biggest of the bunch, but the novelty will quickly wear off once you start cooking and the desired flavor isn't quite there. Whether you're selecting your main ingredient from a farmers' market or from the garden, try to pick squash that are on the small side (about 8 inches long or less), blemish-free and brightly colored. The larger squash grow, the harder, seedier and paler they become.

Tropical Zucchini Ice Cream

There might not be any sweet in the world that's more unnecessarily avoided by home cooks than ice cream. The main concern: Tempering eggs into a custard. This egg-free ice cream might not be quite as decadent as its egg-possessing counterparts, but it's every bit as creamy and a perfect jumping off point for folks who have been timid about crafting their own frozen creations at home. "Tropical" and "zucchini" don't usually land in the same sentence, but this ice cream tastes like the best island vacation you've ever experienced, full of coconut drinks, Beach Boys sing-alongs and snacking on fresh fruits and vegetables.

- One 14-ounce can sweetened condensed milk
- 1 cup unsweetened coconut milk
- ¼ cup pineapple juice
- ½ teaspoon coconut extract
- ½ cup sugar
- ½ teaspoon salt
- 1 cup coarsely grated zucchini
- ½ cup coconut flakes, unsweetened

In a large bowl, whisk together the sweetened condensed milk, coconut milk, pineapple juice, coconut extract, sugar and salt until combined. Gently fold in the zucchini, cover and refrigerate for 4 hours. After chilling, stir in the coconut flakes, mixing until evenly distributed.

Freeze in an ice cream maker according to the manufacturer's instructions, then chill for 2 hours longer before serving.

Summer Squash Ceviche with Ginger Cashew Crumble

Developing squash recipes that focus on heat-free preparations means a deep dive into the world of raw and vegan. This take on "ceviche" constantly surprises people with its crispness, freshness and versatility. The trick is ensuring that the squash is sliced paper-thin (best accomplished with a mandoline) so it can absorb all the citrusy, garlicky marinade. It's also a visually stunning centerpiece for any type of outdoor dining, with jewel-toned hues that are so pretty they're almost romantic.

½ pound summer squash, thinly sliced using a mandoline (or your best knife skills)

2 medium carrots, cut into matchsticks (about 1 cup)

2 tablespoons roughly chopped cilantro

¼ cup fresh lime juice

3 tablespoons minced garlic

¼ cup olive oil

1 tablespoon salt plus ½ teaspoon salt, divided

½ teaspoon red pepper flakes

1 cup whole cashews, toasted

2 tablespoons finely grated ginger

1 tablespoon finely grated lemon zest

½ teaspoon fresh lemon juice

1 blood orange, segmented, for garnish

serves 8

Place the squash and carrots in a large, shallow dish. In a small bowl, combine the cilantro, lime juice, garlic, olive oil, 1 tablespoon of the salt and the red pepper flakes. Pour the mixture over the vegetables and stir so that all the slices and matchsticks are covered. Let marinate at room temperature for 20 minutes.

Meanwhile, combine the cashews, ginger, remaining ½ teaspoon of salt, lemon zest and juice in a food processor and pulse until pebbly.

Divide the ceviche and marinade among bowls. Top with the blood orange segments and cashew crumble and serve immediately.

Green Garden Marys

Vegetables in cocktails are usually limited to martini olives and the almighty tomato-based Bloody Mary. Here, I let zucchini take a crack at the spotlight in this incredibly spicy, steam-from-the-nose concoction. If you're looking to tamp down the heat a bit, omit the serrano pepper. If you want to avoid booze, leave out the vodka, and you'll have a clean, green juice waiting to greet you after a yoga class.

3 medium green tomatoes, cut into quarters

2 medium zucchini (about ⅔ pound), peeled and sliced into 1-inch chunks

1 tablespoon fresh lemon juice

¼ cup fresh cilantro leaves, chopped

1 jalapeño, halved and seeded

½ green bell pepper, stem and seeds removed

½ serrano pepper, seeded and diced

1 teaspoon Worcestershire sauce

Salt and freshly ground black pepper

9 ounces vodka

Zucchini spears, for garnish

In a blender, combine the tomatoes, zucchini, lemon juice, cilantro, peppers, ¾ cup of water and the Worcestershire sauce. Blend well, then strain through a fine-mesh sieve set over a large bowl; discard the solids. Season to taste with salt and pepper. Combine 5 ounces of the juice with 1½ ounces vodka in an ice-filled glass and stir; repeat to make 6 drinks. Garnish with the zucchini spears and serve.

Zucchini Pasta with Pink-Peppercorn Vinaigrette

Another raw dish that will save you from slaving over a hot stove in the (already-scorching) summer heat, this zucchini-based take on a panzanella salad is crisp, bright and almost healthy enough to be called a spa meal. (Also, you have to promise me you'll never call these zucchini noodles "zoodles" because it just makes us all feel bad. Promise? Okay, good.)

⅓ cup freshly grated Parmesan cheese

¼ cup plus 2 tablespoons olive oil, divided

1 tablespoon fresh lemon juice

2 teaspoons pink peppercorns

1 teaspoon minced garlic

Salt

½ small loaf sourdough, cut into 1-inch cubes (about 3 cups)

2 cups julienned zucchini (or cut using a spiralizer)

2 teaspoons capers

In a food processor, combine the Parmesan, ¼ cup of the oil, lemon juice, peppercorns, garlic and ½ teaspoon of salt and pulse a few times until the peppercorns are completely incorporated. Transfer to a bowl and set aside.

In a large skillet, heat the remaining 2 tablespoons of oil until it glistens. Add the bread and cook over low heat, stirring frequently, until golden brown all over, about 10 minutes.

In a serving bowl, toss the zucchini and vinaigrette until combined. Add the croutons and toss gently until evenly distributed. Sprinkle with the capers and serve immediately. Store any leftover croutons in an airtight container.

Savory Squash Clafoutis

This age-old dessert from the Limousin region of France embodies the kind of understated elegance that makes people ooh and aah with its pops of color and creamy texture. Traditionally made with black cherries (which leak almond-flavored juices during the baking process), this savory squash version is equally rustic but fuses together the freshness of zucchini and rosemary with the smoky bite of aged cheddar and tart-sweetness of balsamic-soaked pears.

---

serves **6** *to* **8**

1 tablespoon melted butter, for greasing the pan

1 Bosc pear

1½ teaspoons balsamic vinegar

3 large eggs

1 cup heavy cream

1 cup all-purpose flour

1 teaspoon salt

½ teaspoon freshly ground black pepper

3 teaspoons minced fresh rosemary

⅓ cup coarsely grated aged white cheddar cheese

¾ cup coarsely grated zucchini, drained

Preheat the oven to 375°. Grease a 9-inch ovenproof pie pan with the melted butter. Using a mandoline (or your best knife skills), slice the pear into paper-thin fans; they should be almost translucent. Place the pear slices in a shallow bowl with the vinegar and let marinate while you assemble the remainder of the dish.

In a large bowl, whisk together the eggs and cream. Add the flour, salt, pepper, rosemary and cheese and stir until combined. Gently fold in the zucchini and pour the batter into the pan. Drain the pear slices, allowing the excess vinegar to drip off, then arrange the fans in a ring on top of the custard. Bake until the custard is set and a knife inserted comes out clean, about 40 minutes. Let the clafoutis cool for an hour and serve.

Summer Squash Muffins

Over the past couple of decades, muffins have been bastardized in so many ways, with stumps and tops removed from one another and sizes that have grown to gargantuan proportions. (Paging Elaine Benes!) These squash muffins are a return to the pastry's roots. They combine the zest of ginger, earthiness of almond and tartness of dried cranberries with summer squash to create a sweet-savory balance that's perfect for an early morning breakfast or dinner roll replacement. If you can't find crème fraîche, use sour cream in its place.

For the muffins:

½ cup crème fraîche

½ cup (1 stick) unsalted butter, melted

1 teaspoon honey

½ teaspoon almond extract

1 large egg plus 1 yolk

½ cup light brown sugar

1 tablespoon baking powder

1½ cups all-purpose flour

½ teaspoon salt

1 tablespoon ground ginger

1½ teaspoons ground cloves

1 cup grated summer squash

¼ cup candied ginger, minced

½ cup dried cranberries

For the streusel topping:

½ cup slivered almonds

½ cup (1 stick) unsalted butter, softened

½ cup light brown sugar

1 tablespoon ground ginger

Preheat the oven to 400°. Grease a 12-cup muffin tin with nonstick cooking spray.

Make the muffin batter: In a medium bowl, whisk together the crème fraîche, butter, honey, almond extract, egg and egg yolk until completely combined.

In a large bowl, whisk together the sugar, baking powder, flour, salt, ginger and cloves until combined. Add the wet ingredients to the dry, whisking until completely incorporated (the batter will be very thick).

Fold the squash, ginger and cranberries into the batter until evenly distributed. Using a large tablespoon, scoop the batter into the prepared tin so that each cup is about halfway full.

Make the streusel: Place the almonds, butter, sugar and ginger in a large bowl and stir until completely combined and slightly crumbly.

Sprinkle each muffin with some of the streusel and bake until golden brown, about 20 minutes. Let the muffins cool for 30 minutes before removing them from the tin. They will keep up to 3 days stored in an airtight container.

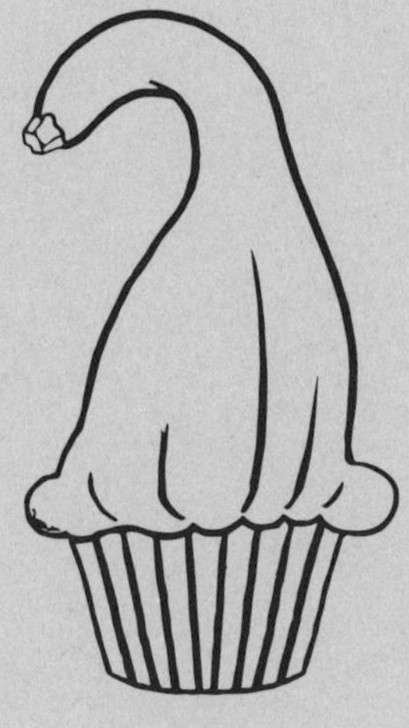

Double-Chocolate Zucchini Cake

We all know and love zucchini bread, but there's something even more special about the kind of cake you can (and should) eat for breakfast. This double-chocolate zucchini creation is charming in its simplicity, fusing together a potluck-ready, crowd-pleasing cake and quasi-healthy zucchini bread. The trick is to very gingerly fold in the zucchini and refrain from overmixing, which will render your cake more gummy than tender. For those looking to double up on the boozy flavor, substitute a chocolate stout in place of the brewed coffee for a malty kick.

For the chocolate cake:

½ cup (1 stick) unsalted butter, softened, plus more for greasing the pan

1½ cups light-brown sugar

2 large eggs

¼ cup sunflower oil

2¼ cups all-purpose flour

½ cup unsweetened cocoa powder

1 teaspoon baking soda

¼ teaspoon salt

1 teaspoon ground cinnamon

1 teaspoon allspice

1 cup brewed coffee, cooled

2 cups coarsely grated zucchini

1 cup bittersweet (70%) chocolate chunks

For the frosting:

½ cup (1 stick) unsalted butter, softened

2 cups confectioner's sugar

2 tablespoons plus 1½ teaspoons bourbon

1 teaspoon pure vanilla extract

Make the cake: Preheat the oven to 375°. Grease a 10-inch cake pan with butter and set aside.

Using a handheld mixer, cream the butter and sugar in a medium bowl at medium speed until light and fluffy, about 5 minutes. In a separate small bowl, beat the eggs and oil with the hand mixer until silky, about 2 minutes.

In a large bowl, whisk together the flour, cocoa powder, baking soda, salt, cinnamon and allspice. Alternating between the butter mixture and the egg mixture, add the wet ingredients to the dry, beating after each addition with the hand mixer until completely incorporated.

Add the coffee, beating a final time with the mixer until the batter is glossy.

Using a wooden spatula, fold in the zucchini and chocolate chunks. Pour the batter into the prepared cake pan and transfer to the middle rack of the oven. Bake for 55 minutes, rotating the halfway through, or until a knife inserted in the center comes out clean.

Remove the cake from the oven and invert onto a wire rack. Let the cake cool for 1 hour.

While the cake is cooling, make the frosting: Beat the butter and sugar until light and creamy, about 5 minutes. Fold in the bourbon and vanilla, mixing until combined. Let the frosting rest for 1 hour, then spread it evenly on the cooled cake. The cake can be stored in an airtight container for up to 5 days.

What about Cucumbers?

In spite of similar appearances and common misconception (both are actually fruit, not vegetables), cucumbers are not members of the squash family. Also, zucchini and cucumbers can't cross-pollinate to create a weird, super pickling hybrid. Sorry, mad scientists.)

Ratatouille Galettes

I've been accused (on more than one occasion) of loving things that are slightly twee. I resisted the characterization for a long time (while listening to Belle and Sebastian and wearing Peter Pan collars, of course), but I've finally come to accept it. If it's cute, tiny or cute and tiny, I'm probably going to fall in love. These personal-size galettes might not reach Zooey-Deschanel-playing-the-ukulele levels of cuteness, but they are charmingly sized and festively colored, with a sauce of cherry tomatoes, garlic and walnuts topped with petals of zucchini and summer squash. Grinding the sesame seeds into the dough is essential so that the crust has a welcome additional crackle. If you're looking for a more sesame-seed-dappled look, knead in another ½ teaspoon of whole seeds before chilling the dough.

For the crust:

1¾ cups all-purpose flour

½ teaspoon salt

¼ cup (½ stick) cold unsalted butter, cut into cubes

1 tablespoon sesame seeds

½ cup heavy cream, chilled

For the filling:

1 cup cherry tomatoes

2 garlic cloves

½ cup raw walnuts

½ cup sliced red onion

½ teaspoon salt

1 medium zucchini (about 7 ounces), sliced into ¼-inch rounds

1 medium summer squash (about 6 ounces), sliced into ¼-inch rounds

½ teaspoon dried basil or dried parsley

1 egg white

Make the crust: In a food processor, pulse the flour, salt, butter and sesame seeds until the mixture forms a coarse meal. With the machine running, slowly add the cream until it's been completely incorporated. Pulse until the dough begins to pull away from the sides of the processor and form a ball. Transfer the dough to a clean surface and form into a 2-inch-thick disc. Cover with plastic and refrigerate for 2 hours. Preheat the oven to 400°.

Make the filling: In a food processor, combine the tomatoes, garlic, walnuts and onion and pulse until chunky.

Assemble the galettes: Divide the dough into four equal pieces and roll each one out into a 6-inch round about ¼-inch thick.

Spread a tablespoon of tomato mixture in the center of each round (kind of like a pizza), leaving a 1-inch margin on all sides. Arrange 3 to 4 slices (total) of zucchini and summer squash in the center of each round on top of the sauce. Fold the dough's overhang in toward the center, pleating it as you go. Brush the dough edges with the egg white and sprinkle each galette with some of the basil or parsley.

Transfer the galettes to a baking sheet and bake until the crust is golden brown, about 40 minutes. Let cool on a rack for 5 minutes, then serve.

Prepping Your Squash

Squash is, by its very nature, full of water and often requires draining to remove excess moisture. Using salt as a coaxing mechanism is often the best way to simultaneously draw out water that would otherwise render a dish soggy while retaining the textural integrity of the squash.

Roasted Squash Trifle with Fennel-Pecan Pesto & Whipped Goat Cheese

Trifles are always a sight to behold and make an ideal centerpiece for any celebration. This savory play on the British classic (a dessert staple since 1596) combines roasted squash, tangy goat cheese and the unexpectedly complementary pairing of buttery pecans and licorice-tinged fennel whipped into a thick pesto. If you're not a goat cheese fan (or even if you are), try experimenting with cotija or dry curd cottage cheese in its place.

For the pesto:

1 bunch fennel fronds (about 1 lightly packed cup)

¼ cup pecans, toasted

⅓ cup grated Parmesan cheese

½ teaspoon rice wine vinegar

½ teaspoon fresh lemon juice

½ cup olive oil

For the squash:

¾ pound yellow squash, cut into 1-inch cubes (about 2 cups)

2 teaspoons olive oil

1 teaspoon salt

½ teaspoon freshly ground black pepper

1 teaspoon garlic, minced

For the goat cheese:

10 ounces goat cheese, softened

6 tablespoons half-and-half

1½ teaspoons ground coriander

¼ teaspoon salt

¼ teaspoon freshly ground black pepper

Make the pesto: In a food processor, pulse the fennel fronds, pecans and Parmesan a few times until the mixture forms a coarse meal. With the motor running, slowly drizzle in the vinegar, followed by the lemon juice and oil until the mixture forms a thick paste.

Make the goat cheese: Using an electric mixer, combine the goat cheese, half-and-half, coriander, salt and pepper and beat at medium speed until fluffy, about 2 minutes.

Make the squash: Preheat the oven to 400°. In a large bowl, mix the cubed squash with the oil, salt, pepper and garlic. Spread evenly in a roasting pan and cook until the squash is fork-tender, about 20 minutes. Let cool completely.

Assemble the trifle: In individual jelly jars or 8-ounce glasses, layer the cooled squash, goat cheese and pesto until the jar or glass is filled, ending with the goat cheese layer on top. Serve immediately.

Old Bay Egg-in-the-Squash

I have a deep affection for the childhood breakfast classic toad-in-the-hole (aka egg-in-the-hole or eggs-in-a-basket). This squash-centered take celebrates the often-overlooked gem squash, which has found the majority of its popularity in roasted or grilled form but is slowly winding its way into the repertoires of squash-loving cooks in other applications. This dish also celebrates Old Bay, a seaside seasoning beloved by East Coasters for decades but rarely used with vegetables or, really, any critter that didn't emerge from the water. With this dish, no one puts gem squash or Old Bay in the corner. If gem squash is hard to come by, any squash that allows itself to serve as a tiny cooking pot will work in a pinch.

serves 2

- 1 large gem squash (about 10 ounces)
- 2 tablespoons unsalted butter, melted
- 3 teaspoons kosher salt
- 3 teaspoons pepper
- 2 teaspoons Old Bay seasoning
- 2 large eggs
- 2 teaspoons garlic, minced
- 1 teaspoon grated Manchego cheese, plus more for serving

Trim ½ inch from the tip and tail ends of the squash so that both sides can sit flat on a baking sheet. Halve the squash across the middle horizontally. Scoop out the seeds, leaving ½-inch margin of squash flesh.

Brush each interior of the squash halves with 1 tablespoon of butter and sprinkle with salt, pepper and Old Bay. Place the squash on a greased baking sheet and bake until it's fork-tender, about 20 minutes.

Remove the baking sheet from the oven. Crack a whole egg into the center of each squash half, and sprinkle the eggs with half of the garlic and cheese. Reduce the oven temperature to 375°, and bake until the egg whites are set but the yolks are still runny, about 18 minutes. Sprinkle with additional cheese, if desired, and serve immediately.

Lamb-Stuffed Pattypan Squash

This dish almost feels like dining on jewelry, with edible baubles of woodsy lamb, pearls of Israeli couscous and quartz-like chunks of feta inside a pattypan treasure chest. (Who can resist such an adorable, sparkplug vegetable anyway?) The dish is perfect for both groups and solo dining, and it has a filling that freezes beautifully and can be easily thawed. Currants will work if sultanas are hard to come by, but sultanas bring a plumpness and sweetness to the dish that bursts forth with juicy pops of color and flavor.

8 small pattypan squash

1 tablespoon olive oil

Salt and freshly ground black pepper

2 tablespoons sesame oil

3 tablespoons minced garlic

1 tablespoon plus 1½ teaspoons caraway seeds

1 pound ground lamb

1 cup (dry) Israeli couscous, cooked according to the package instructions

1 cup crumbled feta

3 tablespoons sultanas

Preheat the oven to 350°. Cut off the stem and top of each squash so the interior is exposed and scoop out the seeds, leaving a ½-inch thickness of flesh inside. Rub the inside and outside of each squash with olive oil and sprinkle with salt and pepper.

Heat the sesame oil in a large skillet over medium heat. Add the garlic and cook until soft, about 1 minute. Add the caraway seeds and cook for another minute. Add the lamb, cooking until browned, about 8 minutes. Remove the mixture from heat and let it cool. Stir in the couscous and feta.

Fill each squash with the lamb mixture. Arrange the squash in a glass baking dish and add ½ inch of water. Bake until the squash is fork-tender, about 25 minutes. Sprinkle with the sultanas and extra feta if desired. Serve immediately. Freeze any leftover filling.

Tokfozelek (Hungarian Squash & Dill Casserole)

My grandmother grew up in a mining town in Southern Illinois, and while our heritage is freckle-faced Irish through and through, Hungarian influences ran deep within the community and throughout her cooking. This dill-flavored (no really, it's all dill, all the time) side dish isn't anything showy, but it's the kind of hearty comfort food that sneaks up on you with a welcome acidic kick added by the mellowness of sour cream. If you're giving a dinner party and feeling particularly fancy, serve the dish in individual ramekins. Plus, saying *tokfozelek* five times fast is a party trick in of itself.

serves **6**

- 2 cups coarsely grated summer squash
- 1½ teaspoons salt
- 2 tablespoons sherry vinegar
- 1 tablespoon plus 1½ teaspoons finely chopped fresh dill, plus more for garnish
- 1 tablespoon dill pickle juice
- 1 teaspoon ground dill weed
- ½ teaspoon chopped tarragon
- 1 tablespoon onion powder
- 2 tablespoons unsalted butter
- ⅓ cup sour cream
- 2 tablespoons all-purpose flour
- 3 teaspoons hot paprika, plus more for garnish

Place the squash in a colander over a sink or large bowl and sprinkle with the salt. Let the squash drain for 2 to 3 hours.

In a Dutch oven, combine the squash, vinegar, dill, pickle juice, dill weed, tarragon, onion powder and butter. Cover and cook over medium-high heat until the squash is tender, about 12 minutes.

In a small bowl, combine the sour cream, flour and paprika. Add to the Dutch oven, stirring until the flour is completely integrated and the dish has thickened, about 4 to 5 minutes. Sprinkle with chopped dill and paprika and serve immediately.

Summer Squash Cobbler

This is far and away the most winter-appropriate dish in this book, and the in-your-face flavors (blue cheese! sage! roasted tomatoes!) might seem as though they'd overshadow the lowly squash. But squash stealthily steals the spotlight, taking in all the nuance of its bolder counterparts and slowly simmering behind the scenes until bursting forth like a culinary Gypsy Rose Lee under a fluffy bed of drop biscuits. It's important to remember that drop biscuits in their uncooked form are downright ugly, particularly when they have so many glorious, chunky ingredients in play. In this case, the ugly duckling quickly becomes a delicious swan.

For the biscuits:

2 cups all-purpose flour

1 teaspoon salt

1 tablespoon plus 1½ teaspoons baking powder

6 tablespoons cold unsalted butter, cubed

1¼ cups heavy cream

½ teaspoon freshly ground black pepper

½ teaspoon ground sage

2 teaspoons finely grated Parmesan cheese

½ cup coarsely grated Manchego cheese

For the cobbler:

¼ cup olive oil

1 pound summer squash, sliced into half-moons (about 3 cups)

1 small Vidalia onion, minced (about ¾ cup)

2 teaspoons minced garlic

1 cup cherry tomatoes

½ cup chicken stock

1 tablespoon fresh lemon juice

¼ cup all-purpose flour

½ teaspoon black pepper

½ cup crumbled blue cheese

Make the biscuit dough: In a food processor, combine the flour, salt, and baking powder, pulsing until evenly distributed. Add the butter one tablespoon at a time and pulse until the mixture becomes a coarse meal.

Scrape the dough into a bowl and stir in the cream, pepper, sage and Parmesan. Fold in the Manchego and knead until the dough holds together. Wrap the dough in plastic and refrigerate for 2 hours.

Preheat the oven to 400°. Grease an 8-inch-square baking dish.

Make the cobbler: In a large skillet, heat the oil over medium heat until glistening. Add the squash and onion and cook until the squash starts to become tender and the onion begins to soften, about 7 minutes. Add the garlic and cherry tomatoes and cook, stirring, until the tomatoes have burst, 4 to 5 minutes.

In a small bowl, whisk together the chicken stock, lemon juice, flour and pepper. Stir this mixture into the vegetables and increase the heat to high. Let the mixture cook until the flour has been completely incorporated, about 3 minutes. Pour the contents of the pan into the baking dish. Sprinkle with the blue cheese.

Using an ice cream scoop or large spoon, top the vegetables with spoonfuls of biscuit dough, about 6 to 8 large lumps for the pan. Bake until the biscuit topping is golden brown, about 30 minutes. Serve immediately.

Apple-Zucchini Latkes with Thyme-Honey Butter

These spicy, lightly honeyed latkes have become my go-to Sunday brunch staple. They're low-fuss enough to make with kids or toss together when you're feeling the effects of one-too-many cocktails from the night before. (There's also a beautiful moment of wringing out all the water from the zucchini and apples that always makes me feel like a rustic pioneer woman.) The sherry is key: It marries the spices, zucchini and apples while providing a little "hair of the dog" nip. What's more, I downright adore compound butters, and think that their ease of preparation and ability to elevate a dish is completely underrated. Rolling the butter into a 1-inch-wide sausage-like link allows for slivers to be shaved off with just the right density.

1 large zucchini (about 10 oz.), peeled and coarsely grated

2 medium, tart apples (such as Granny Smith)—peeled, cored and coarsely grated

¾ cup rice flour

1 egg plus 1 egg white

1 teaspoon Amontillado sherry

1 teaspoon allspice

1 teaspoon cardamom

2 tablespoons unsalted butter, plus more as needed

Thyme-Honey Butter, for serving (recipe follows)

Place the zucchini and apple in a clean kitchen towel and fold it into a roll. Hold on to either end of the towel and twist to squeeze out the excess water. Repeat if necessary, then place the mixture in a large bowl.

In a small bowl, whisk together the flour, egg, egg white, sherry and spices. Add to the zucchini-apple mixture and stir to combine. Let the batter rest for 15 minutes.

In a cast-iron skillet, heat the butter until melted and glistening. Ladle tablespoons of batter into the butter about 1 inch apart and flatten with the backside of the spoon. Fry on each side until golden brown, about 2 minutes per side. Drain the latkes on paper towels, then transfer them to a platter. Repeat with the remaining latke mixture, adding more butter (1 tablespoon at a time) as needed.

Serve the latkes warm with slices of thyme-honey butter.

Thyme-Honey Butter

½ cup (1 stick) unsalted butter, at room temperature

1 tablespoon chopped thyme

1 tablespoon clover honey

In a medium bowl, mix all the ingredients together until evenly distributed. Ladle the butter mixture onto a square of plastic wrap or wax paper and roll it into a log approximately 1 inch across. Refrigerate until firm.

Curried Squash Hush Puppies with Ricotta-Mint Dip

Across the South, a debate rages about whether biscuits or hush puppies are the perfect sidekick to fried fish and melty macaroni and cheese. I'll stay mum about my opinion on the topic,* but these squash-laced, tender hush puppies punched up with a shake of curry powder might be game changers for even the most diehard biscuit devotees. The ricotta sauce is made more for dipping and dunking than drizzling, and it serves as a minty foil that's the perfect cooling agent for the hush puppies' steamy (almost sultry) flavor profile.

*No I won't; I'm a hush puppy girl.

½ pound summer squash, cut into 1-inch cubes

(1½ cups)

½ cup buttermilk

½ cup self-rising cornmeal

½ cup all-purpose flour

1 teaspoon sea salt

1 teaspoon black pepper

1½ teaspoons curry powder

1 large egg, beaten

½ cup finely diced shallots

Canola oil, for frying

Ricotta-Mint Dip, for serving (recipe follows)

In a heavy-bottomed pot fitted with a colander, bring 2 inches of water to a boil. When the water begins to boil, place the squash in the colander, cover and cook until it's completely tender, about 5 minutes. Let the squash drain for 30 minutes over a sink or empty bowl, lightly pressing with a spatula once to push out any additional water.

In a large bowl, whisk together the buttermilk, cornmeal, flour, salt, pepper and curry powder. Add the egg and mix until combined. Fold in the squash and shallots.

In a large heavy-bottomed pot, heat 2 inches of oil until it reaches 350° on a deep-fry thermometer. Working in batches of four or five, use a melon baller to scoop rounds of batter into the oil. Fry until golden brown on all sides, about 5 minutes. Using a slotted spoon, transfer the hush puppies to a paper-towel-lined plate to drain. Serve immediately alongside the Ricotta-Mint Dip.

Ricotta-Mint Dip

- ½ cup Greek yogurt
- ½ cup ricotta
- 2½ tablespoons finely chopped mint
- 1 tablespoon lemon juice
- 2 tablespoons olive oil
- 2 teaspoons minced garlic

Place a fine-mesh strainer fitted with cheesecloth over a large bowl. Add the Greek yogurt and let it strain for 15 minutes. Place the strained yogurt in a small bowl with all the other ingredients and whisk until combined. Chill for 1 hour, stirring occasionally, or until ready to serve. The dip can be prepared up to 12 hours in advance and refrigerated until ready to use.

Deep-Fried Squash Blossoms

Squash blossoms provide us with an opportunity to tackle a topic that's not often covered in cookbooks: vegetable sex education. Ready, class? Squash blossoms come in both "male" and "female" genders, with only "female" blossoms growing into full vegetables. (You can happily munch on as many of these male blossoms as you want without feeling guilty that you've deprived them of a rich life as a full-grown squash.) Male squash blossoms are flashy, dangling out on the edges of the plant, and have a long interior stamen (no dirty jokes, please). Female squash blossoms grow toward the middle of the plant and are more pod-like, waiting to be pollinated through a song-and-dance between the male flowers and buzzy bees. For cooking purposes, it's important to remember that male blossoms keep longer than female blossoms (a couple of days versus a few hours). In order to clean the supple, tender male squash blossoms for stuffing in this recipe, remove the four-pronged stamen from the interior of the flower with a swift pluck and rinse thoroughly to remove any bugs or dirt. These deep-fried squash blossoms are sweet, not savory, and contain a cane-syrup-and-mascarpone filling that's perfectly treacle-y. If cane syrup isn't available in your area, sorghum is a fine replacement.

- 1 cup cake flour
- 1 tablespoon plus 1½ teaspoons fresh lemon juice
- ½ teaspoon dark rum
- 1 large egg
- 1 teaspoon light brown sugar
- ¼ cup cane syrup (such as Steen's)
- 1 cup mascarpone cheese
- 10 squash blossoms, washed, stamens and stems removed
- 3 cups canola oil, for frying
- Confectioners' sugar, for dusting

In a medium bowl, whisk together the flour, ½ cup of water, lemon juice and rum until combined. Beat in the egg until it's completely incorporated, followed by the sugar. Let the batter rest at room temperature for 1 hour.

In a heavy-bottomed saucepan, heat 1 inch of oil until it reaches 375° on a deep-fry thermometer.

In a small bowl, fold the cane syrup and mascarpone together until completely combined. Tuck 1 teaspoon of mascarpone filling into each squash blossom, securing the petal end with a gentle twist.

Working in batches of three, dip the blossoms into the batter, shake off the excess, then lower gently into the oil. Cook the blossoms until golden brown on each side, about 1 minute. Using a slotted spoon, transfer the blossoms to paper towels and let drain. Dust lightly with confectioners' sugar and serve immediately.

Squash-Blossom Soup with Poblano Chiles & Crema

Yes, squash blossoms are elegant. Yes, they are flowers that seem too beautiful to ingest. Yes, you might initially feel badly about chopping them up into a soup—but don't. Although the majority of squash-blossom soups are served warm and include a meaty component, this version remains vegetarian and more closely resembles a refreshing gazpacho with a punch of heat from roasted poblano chiles.

1 tablespoon unsalted butter

2 tablespoons minced garlic

1 cup fresh corn kernels

3 cups chopped yellow summer squash

2 cups chopped squash blossoms (about 20 blossoms), plus 8 whole blossoms for garnish

½ teaspoon fresh lemon juice

1 quart heavy cream

½ poblano chile—roasted, peeled and deseeded

½ teaspoon salt

½ teaspoon freshly ground black pepper

1 tablespoon crema or sour cream, for garnish

Heat the butter in a large saucepan over medium heat. Add the garlic and cook, stirring, until aromatic, about 1 minute. Add the corn, squash, chopped squash blossoms, lemon juice and cream and simmer over medium heat until the squash is fork-tender, about 15 minutes.

Transfer the mixture to a food processor along with the chile, salt and pepper. Process until smooth. Strain the soup through a fine-mesh strainer and chill until cooled, about 3 hours. Garnish with squash blossoms and a dollop of crema and serve.

Succotash with Mustard Cream

Succotash is a pan-fried vegetable medley that grew in popularity across rural America at the turn of the 20th century. This side dish might as well hold a tiny sign that reads, "Any and all vegetables are welcome!" Although its popularity has waned most places, succotash has retained a firm foothold in the South. Humble lima beans and sweet corn serve as anchor ingredients, but they're elevated with the back-of the-throat heat of horseradish, tarragon and (of course) squash. This version is cooled and tossed in a mustard-laced cream sauce, making it the ideal accompaniment to barbecue.

serves 6

- 3 tablespoons unsalted butter
- 1 teaspoon finely chopped tarragon
- 1 teaspoon grated horseradish
- 2 cups diced summer squash (about ¾ pound)
- ½ cup edamame, shelled
- ½ cup lima beans
- ½ cup fresh sweet corn kernels
- ½ cup crème fraîche
- 1 tablespoon Dijon mustard
- ½ teaspoon cider vinegar
- ½ teaspoon salt
- ½ teaspoon freshly ground black pepper
- Pine nuts, to garnish (optional)

In a skillet, melt the butter over medium heat. Add the tarragon and horseradish and cook until aromatic, about 2 minutes. Add the squash, edamame, lima beans and corn and cook, stirring, until the squash is fork-tender, 10 to 12 minutes. Remove the vegetables from the heat and transfer to a large bowl.

While the vegetables cool, whisk together the crème fraîche, mustard, vinegar, salt and pepper in a bowl until incorporated. Drizzle the dressing over the vegetables and toss to coat. Garnish with pine nuts, if desired, and serve.

Thank You!

From the bottom of my heart, a thanks to Nick, Kaitlyn and the entire Short Stack team for allowing me the opportunity to place my favorite summertime vegetable on a pedestal.

Special thanks to Joe Jackson's 1982 classic hit "Steppin' Out" for helping me dance through weeks and months in the kitchen with a spring in my step, as well as the legions of friends who attended squash-themed dinner parties, squash-themed brunches and squash-themed shindigs.

The greatest gratitude, though, goes to all the farmers, gardeners and growers across the New Orleans area who provided me with mountains of squash with which to experiment and play.

—Sarah Baird

Share your Short Stack cooking experiences with us
(or just keep in touch) via:

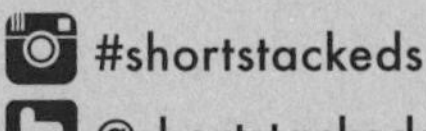

#shortstackeds
@shortstackeds
facebook.com/shortstackeditions
hello@shortstackeditions.com

Colophon

This edition of Short Stack was printed by Circle Press in New York City on Mohawk Britehue Meadow Green (interior) and Neenah Oxford White (cover) paper. The main text of the book is set in Futura and Jensen Pro, and the headlines are set in Lobster.

Sewn by:

Available now at ShortStackEditions.com:

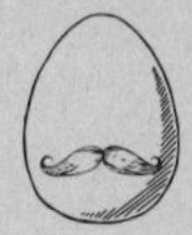

Vol. 1 | Eggs, by Ian Knauer

Vol. 2 | Tomatoes, by Soa Davies

Vol. 3 | Strawberries, by Susan Spungen

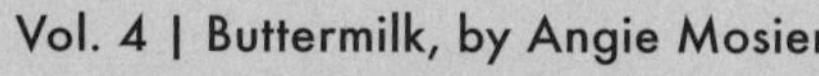

Vol. 4 | Buttermilk, by Angie Mosier

Vol. 5 | Grits, by Virginia Willis

Vol. 6 | Sweet Potatoes, by Scott Hocker

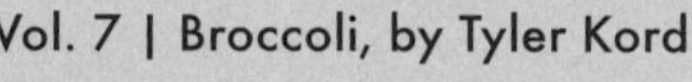

Vol. 7 | Broccoli, by Tyler Kord

Vol. 8 | Honey, by Rebekah Peppler

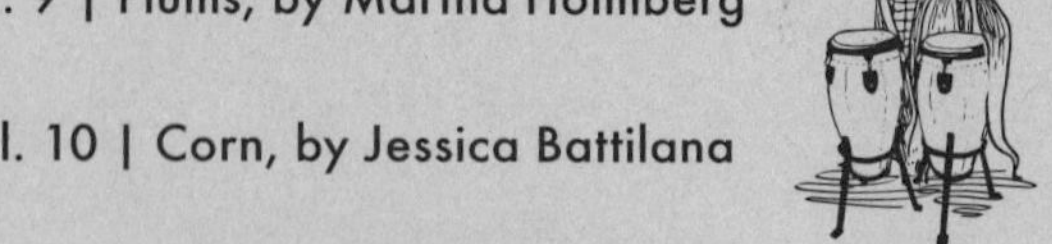

Vol. 9 | Plums, by Martha Holmberg

Vol. 10 | Corn, by Jessica Battilana

Vol. 11 | Apples, by Andrea Albin

Vol. 12 | Brown Sugar, by Libbie Summers

Vol. 13 | Lemons, by Alison Roman

Vol. 14 | Prosciutto di Parma, by Sara Jenkins